Love Holding Love

MANTRAS
DRAWN FROM THE WRITINGS OF
SAINTS FRANCIS AND CLARE OF ASSISI

SONGBOOK

Josef Raischl, SFO

Dedicated to

Georgia and Paul Perkins, SFO,

San Jose, California

Publishers: Josef Raischl, SFO and André Cirino, OFM
Composers: Josef Raischl, SFO, Konrad Raischl, David Dargie
Cover design: Jona Raischl
Original painting:
    Sr. M. Animata Probst, OSF
    Regens Wagner Dillingen
    Prälat-Hummel-Strasse 1
    89407 Dillingen, Germany
    Used with permission.
Sponsor: Paul Perkins, SFO
Original texts of St. Francis: *Opuscula Sancti Patris Francisci Assisiensis*,
ed. by Cajetanus Esser, OFM, Grottaferrata 1978; used with permission.
English text translations and comments:
Frances Teresa Downing, OSC and Murray Bodo, OFM
Spanish: Mary Esther Stewart, Norma V. Mena

Business Manager:
    Mary Esther Stewart
    estherstewart@npgcable.com
    www.arcoirisstudio.com
    Tel. 928-856-9032
Printed and distributed by:
    Tau-publishing
    1422 E. Edgemont Ave.
    Phoenix, AZ 85006
    www.tau-publishing.com
    Tel. 602-625-6183

Table Of Contents

Introduction

Spirituality describes the way a person chooses to relate to God. Francis, Clare and Bonaventure—all saints—are first of all, by their birth, Italians. And Italians are primarily people of the heart. St. Bonaventure, the recognized theologian of St. Francis, names the spirituality that emanates from Francis and Clare to be an affective spirituality, that is, a spirituality of the heart. So he encourages the reader in his meditations on the life of Jesus, the *Tree of Life*, to be able to feel what Mary was feeling at the Annunciation. When writing of the Archangel Gabriel asking Mary to bear God's Son, St. Bonaventure imagines the Holy Spirit descending on her like a divine fire and cries out: "If you could feel that divine fire, if you could hear the Virgin joyfully singing, you too would sing a sweet song."

Franciscan spirituality is an affective spirituality that is rooted in feelings, emotions, experiences of the heart that often get expressed in poetry, sculpture, paintings, music, song and dance. Bonaventure imagines the Virgin joyfully singing at the conception of her child and inviting us to join in this sweet song. So song and music play an integral role in a Franciscan's approach to God.

As you begin to sing these Franciscan mantras, you may begin with voice and perhaps instruments, but as you get into the rhythmic, repetitive singing, then perhaps you will begin to sing from your heart. At the Franciscan sanctuary of Fonte Colombo, above the choir stalls in the main chapel, one reads the following: "Si cor non orat invanum lingua laborat," which translates: "If the heart does not pray, in vain does the tongue labor," or more colloquially, if you don't pray from the heart, then in vain do your lips flap! Therefore, it is our hope that these nuggets of wisdom chosen from the writings of these two great Umbrian saints will become your heart prayers.

This songbook contains all that is needed to accompany the muscial CD, *Love Holding Love:* Mantras Drawn from the Writings of Saints Francis and Clare of Assisi.

It is our belief and experience that rhythmic, repetitive singing will enable those who use these mantras to experience the burning love Francis and Clare had for God, for Jesus Christ. For this reason, we have chosen to present several texts in their original languages of composition: Latin, Italian, and Umbrian dialect, the language of Francis and Clare. Five of the mantras are sung in English and Spanish. It is our hope that this songbook be used by musicians as well as for congregational singing, or simply for personal prayer.

The improvisations heard on the CD are not included because they are alive only in the mind and heart of Konrad Raischl. Musicians are welcome to listen and replicate.

Peace and every good!

Josef Raischl SFO & André Cirino OFM
Feast of St. Francis, 4th October 2008

Third Letter of St. Clare to St. Agnes of Prague (1238)

Our amazement at God's goodness and love for us is echoed by the whole of creation. It is our task to give voice to the inner heart of Brother Sun and Sisters Moon and Stars, and here we see Clare doing just that.

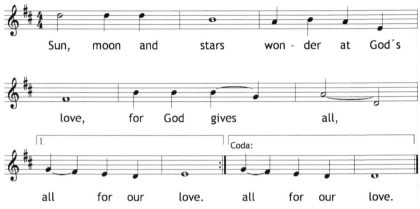

Sun, moon and stars won - der at God's love, for God gives all, all for our love. all for our love.

Text: St. Clare of Assisi
Translation: Frances T. Downing, OSC

Music: Josef Raischl, SFO
Choral arrangement: Josef Raischl, SFO, David Dargie

Sun, moon and stars won-der at God's love
for God gives all, all for our

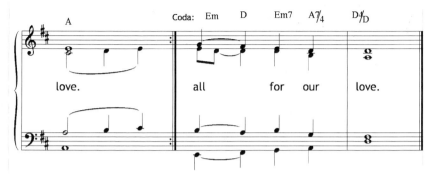

love.　　all　　for　our　love.

Text: St. Clare of Assisi

Music: Josef Raischl, SFO

Translation: Mary Esther Stewart, Norma Mena

Choral arrangement: Josef Raischl, SFO, David Dargie

Sol, lu-na y estre-llas a-la-ban a Dios,

pues Dios da to - do por nues-tro a-

mor.　　por nues - tro a - mor.

Altissimo Glorioso Dio

Opuscula, p. 224; translation and commentary by Murray Bodo, OFM

St. Francis' Prayer before the Crucifix *(1205/06)*

Most High, glorious God, enlighten the darkness of my heart.
Give me right faith, and sure hope, and perfect love,
with understanding and knowledge, O Lord,
to fulfill Your holy and true command.

When Francis first experiences God's grace, he feels that his twenty-five years have been squandered, and he implores his Most High God to change his heart by giving him the faith, hope, and love he needs so as to know how to fulfill God's holy will.

Text: St. Francis of Assisi

Music: Josef Raischl, SFO
Choral arrangement: Josef Raischl, SFO, David Dargie

ALTISSIMU SIGNORE
Opuscula, pp. 84-86; translation by Eric Doyle, OFM [used with permission, Franciscan International Study Centre, Canterbury, England]; commentary by Murray Bodo, OFM

St. Francis' CANTICLE OF THE CREATURES *(1225)*

Most high, all-powerful, good Lord.
Yours are the praise, the glory and the honour and every blessing.
To You alone, Most High, they are due,
and no one is worthy to mention You.

Be praised, my Lord, with all Your creatures, above all Sir Brother Sun,
who is day and by him You shed light upon us.
And he is beautiful and radiant with great splendour,
of You, Most High, he bears the likeness.

Be praised, my Lord, through Sister Moon and the Stars,
in the heavens You have formed them,
clear and precious and beautiful.

Be praised, my Lord, through Brother Wind,
and through Air and Cloud and fair and all Weather,
by which You give nourishment to Your creatures.

Be praised, my Lord, through Sister Water,
who is very useful and humble and precious and pure.

Be praised, my Lord, through Brother Fire,
by whom You light up the night,
and he is beautiful and merry and vigorous and strong.

Be praised, my Lord, through our Sister Mother Earth,
who sustains and directs us,
and produces diverse fruits with coloured flowers and herbs.

Be praised, my Lord, by those who pardon for Your love,
and endure sickness and trials.
Blessed are they who shall endure them in peace,
for by You, Most High, they shall be crowned

Be praised, my Lord, through our Sister Bodily Death,
from whom no one living can escape.
Woe to those who die in mortal sin.
Blessed are those whom she will find in Your most holy will,
for the second death will do them no harm.

Praise and bless my Lord,
and give Him thanks and serve Him with great humility.

Francis sings his CANTICLE in the Umbrian dialect instead of Latin, thus composing the first great Italian poem. The very sounds of his words articulate the intensity of his love and praise for God made manifest in all God's creatures.

Text: St. Francis of Assisi

Music: Josef Raischl, SFO
Choral arrangement: Josef Raischl, SFO

qua-l'è ior-no et al - lu-mi-ni noi per lo- i.

2. Lau-da-to si e mi sign-o - re, per so-ra lu-na e le stel - le, in

ce - lu l'ài for-ma - te cla-ri-te, pre-tios' et bel - le.

3. Lau-da-to si - e mi sign - o - re per fra-te ven - to et per

a - er - e et nu-bi-lo et se-re-no et om-ne tem-po per lo

qua-le al e tu-e cre-a-tu-re dai sus - ten-ta - men-to.

4. Lau-da-to si-e mi sign-o - re per sor' a-qua, mul-to u - ti - le

et hu-mi-le et pre-ti-o - sa et ca - - sta.

5. Lau-da-to si - e mi sign-o - re per fra-te fo-cu, per lo

qua - le enn' al - lu - mi - ni la noc - te, ed el - lo è

bel - lo   et io - cun - do et ro - bus-tos' et for - te.

6. Lau-da-to si - e mi sign - o - re per so - ra nos-tra ma-tre

ter - - ra, la qua - le ne sus-ten-ta et go - ver - na, et pro -

du-ce di - ver-si fruc-ti con co-lo-ri-ti flo - ri et her - ba.

7. Lau - da - to si - e mi sign - o - re per quel - li

ke per- don- a - no per'l tu am - or', et sos - ten - go

in - fir-mi - ta - te et tri-bu - la - ti - o - ne.

8. Be-a-ti quel-li ke'l sos-ter-ra- no in pa - - ce,

ka da te, al-tis-si-mo, si - ra-no in-co-ro - na - ti.

St. Francis' SALUTATION OF THE BLESSED VIRGIN MARY *(undated)*

Hail, my Lady, Holy Queen, Mary, Mother of God. You are virgin made church.
The Most Holy Father has chosen you in heaven,
and with his Most Holy Beloved Son and the Holy Spirit he has consecrated you,
so that in you is all fullness of grace and every good.

Hail God's palace, hail God's tabernacle, hail God's house.
Hail God's vesture, hail God's handmaid, hail God's mother.
Hail all you holy virtues poured into believing hearts through the grace and light
of the Holy Spirit to transform unfaithfulness into faithfulness to God.

The depth of Francis' understanding of Mary is evident in this extraordinary description of Mary as Virgin made Church. It crystallizes the
theology of the Virgin Mary as the image of Christ's virgin Church in
which Christ continues to be born.

Text: St. Francis of Assisi
Translation: Murray Bodo, OFM

Music: Josef Raischl, SFO
Choral arrangement: Josef Raischl, SFO

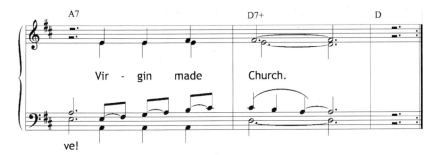

Vir - gin made Church.

ve!

Text: St. Francis of Assisi

Translation: Mary Esther Stewart, Norma Mena

Music: Josef Raischl, SFO

Choral arrangement: Josef Raischl, SFO

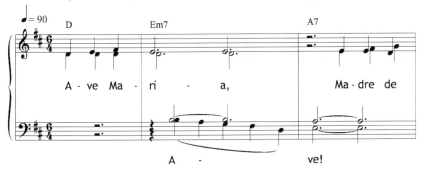

A - ve Ma - rí - a, Ma - dre de

A - ve!

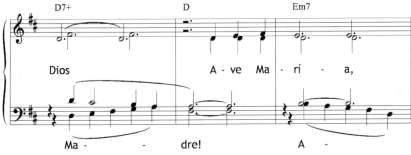

Dios A - ve Ma - rí - a,

Ma - dre! A -

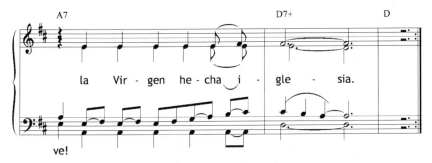

la Vir - gen he - cha i - gle - sia.

ve!

BE TRANSFORMED
Translation and commentary by Frances Teresa Downing, OSC

Third Letter of St. Clare to St. Agnes of Prague (1238)

These may be some of Clare's best known and loved words, her guidance to us as we enter into prayer, her advice to us for loving God and a map which she gives us for the journey into God. This letter was written at a time when Agnes was struggling, and Clare encourages her by recalling the things that really matter.

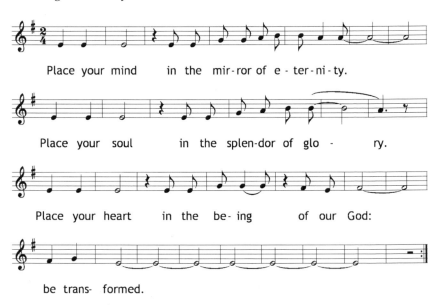

Text: St. Clare of Assisi
Translation: Frances T. Downing, OSC

Music: Josef Raischl, SFO
Choral arrangement: Josef Raischl, SFO, David Dargie

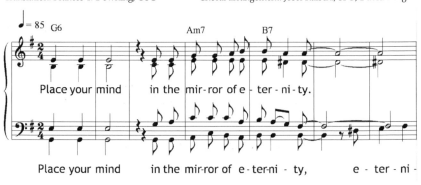

Place your soul in the splen-dor of glo - ry.

Place your soul in the splen-dor of glo' glo - ry.
ty. in the spen-dor of glo - ry.

Place your heart in the be-ing of our God:

Place your heart in the be-ing

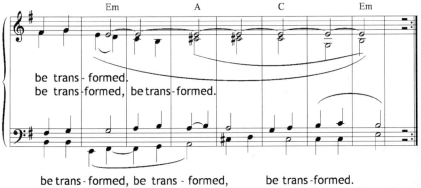

be trans-formed. be trans-formed.
be trans-formed, be trans-formed.

be trans-formed, be trans-formed, be trans-formed.
be trans-formed, be trans-formed, be trans-formed.

Burning Love
Translation and commentary by Frances Teresa Downing, OSC

First Letter of St. Clare to St. Agnes of Prague (1234)

Agnes of Prague is just starting her religious life and Clare writes her a letter encouraging her to risk all for the love of Jesus Christ and to respond to her vocation which was begun by His burning love for Agnes.

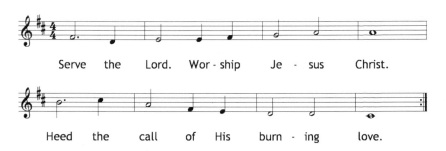

Text: St. Clare of Assisi
Translation: Frances T. Downing, OSC

Music: Josef Raischl, SFO
Choral arrangement: Josef Raischl, SFO, David Dargie

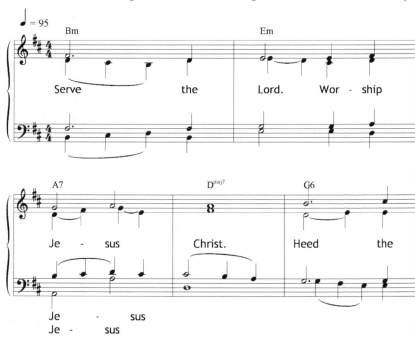

CANTICLE OF THE CREATURES

Translation by Eric Doyle, OFM [used with permission, Franciscan
International Study Centre, Canterbury, England], adapted by
André Cirino, OFM; commentary by Murray Bodo, OFM.

St. Francis' CANTICLE OF THE CREATURES *(1225; see p.9)*

Two years before he dies Francis sings his Swan Song, a song praising
God for and through all God's creatures. The *Canticle* summarizes how
Francis sees the goodness of God in everything God has made.

Text: St. Francis of Assisi

Translation: Eric Doyle, OFM, André Cirino, OFM

Music: Konrad Raischl

Musical adaptation: Josef Raischl, SFO

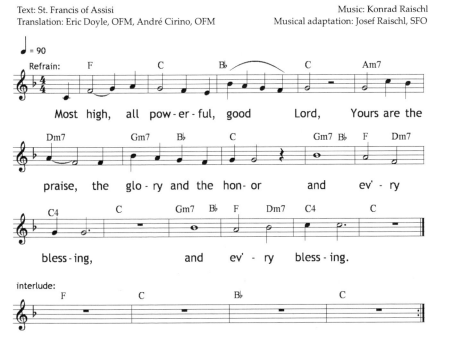

verses:

1. Be praised my Lord, with all Your crea - tures,

a - bove all Sir Broth- er Sun,

who is day, by him you shed light

and he is beau - ti - ful and ra - diant with great splen- dor.

2. Be praised my Lord, through Sis - ter Moon and Stars,

in the heav-ens you´ve formed them clear and pre - cious.

Be praised my Lord, through Broth - er Wind,

and through Air and Cloud and fair and all Weath-er.

3. Be praised my Lord, through Sis - ter Wa - ter,

who is ve - ry use - ful, hum - ble, pre - cious, pure.

Be praised my Lord, through Broth-er Fire,

and he is beau-ti-ful and mer-ry, vi-gor-ous, strong.

4. Be praised my Lord, through Sis-ter Moth-er Earth,

she sus-tains us, with fruits and flow'rs and herbs.

Be praised my Lord, by those who par-don for your love,

and en-dure sick-ness and tri-als.

5. Be praised my Lord, through Sis-ter bo-di-ly Death,

from whom no one liv-ing can es-cape.

Praise and bless and thank my Lord,

and serve God with great hu-mi-li-ty.

Carry Him in Love
Translation and commentary by Murray Bodo, OFM

St. Francis' Second Version of the Letter to the Faithful (1220)

In this extraordinary image from his letter, Francis incarnates the truth that each one of us can conceive and give birth to Christ in our lives, and so carry Him in love.

Text: St. Francis of Assisi/ Translation: Murray Bodo, OFM

Music: Josef Raischl, SFO

Fourth Letter of St. Clare to St. Agnes of Prague (1253)

This was a central theme for Clare, that we can carry our imitation of Mary to the extent of becoming, as she was, one who bears the Word of God, first in our own hearts and then in the hearts of others.

Stay -ing close to Christ's moth-er, hum - ble and poor, we shall

bear our Cre - a - tor whom we a - dore. whom we a - dore.

Text: St. Clare of Assisi

Translation: Frances T. Downing, OSC

Music: David Dargie

Choral arrangement: David Dargie

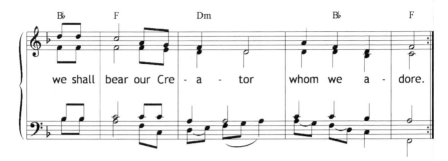

we shall bear our Cre - a - tor whom we a - dore.

DEUS MEUS ET OMNIA
Commentary by Murray Bodo, OFM

LITTLE FLOWERS OF ST. FRANCIS

When the newly-converted Francis stays overnight at the home of Bernard of Quintavalle, Bernard feigns sleep so that he can observe how Francis prays. On his knees Francis prays aloud all night long: *Deus meus et omnia!*—"My God and my all." Bernard is so affected that his heart is changed and he becomes the first follower of Francis.

Text: St. Francis of Assisi

Music: Josef Raischl, SFO
Choral arrangement: Josef Raischl, SFO

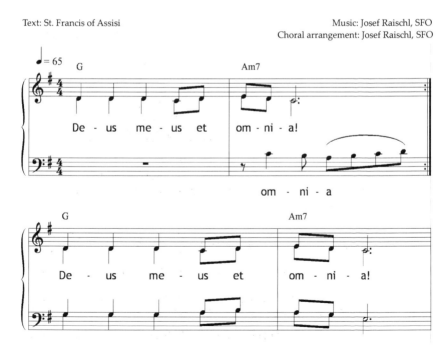

De - us me - us et om - ni - a!

om - ni - a

De - us me - us et om - ni - a!

1. My God and my all!
2. Mein Gott und mein Al - les!
3. Mi Dios y mi to - do!
4. Mon Dieu et mon tout!

De - us me - us et om - ni - a.

5. Di - o mi - o e mi - o tut - to!

FOR THOSE WHO LOVE
Translation and commentary by Frances Teresa Downing, OSC

Third Letter of St. Clare to St. Agnes of Prague (1238)

Clare always seems to speak to the highest and the best in us, so that we go on our way recommitted to the challenge of totally loving the One who has loved us totally.

Taste the sweet - ness hid - den for those who love!

Taste the sweet - ness hid - den for those who love!

Text: St. Clare of Assisi

Translation: Frances T. Downing, OSC

Music: Josef Raischl, SFO

Choral arrangement: Josef Raischl, SFO, David Dargie

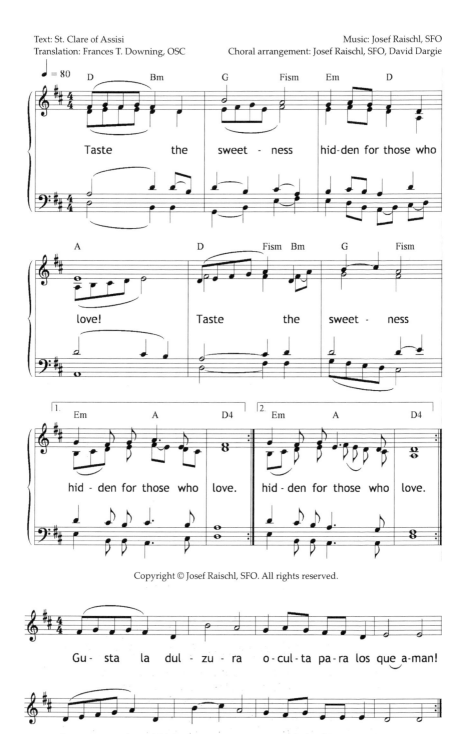

Text: St. Clare of Assisi   Music: Josef Raischl, SFO
Translation: Mary Esther Stewart, Norma Mena   Choral arrangement: Josef Raischl, SFO, David Dargie

FRANCISCAN GREETING
Commentary by Murray Bodo, OFM

Francis continually encourages his brothers to "announce peace to all."
But more than that, they are to affirm the goodness of people, as he
himself does in the mountain village of Poggio Bustone when he
greets the people with *Buon Giorno, buona gente!* "Good morning,
good people!" Peace and Good, *Pax et Bonum*, the Franciscan wish for
everyone.

Text: Traditional Franciscan Greeting

Music: David Dargie
Choral arrangement: David Dargie

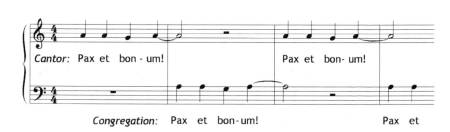

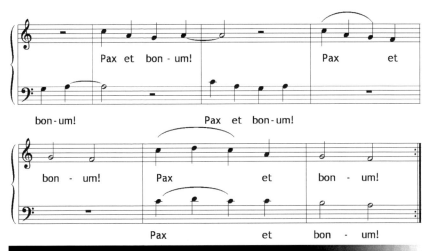

God Alone
Translation and commentary by Murray Bodo, OFM

St. Francis' EARLIER RULE *(1209/10 - 1221)*

Chapter 23 of this Rule has been called a "Franciscan Manifesto." Within that beautiful passage is this poem of Francis' vision of God's essential action in our lives.

Text: St. Francis of Assisi
Translation: Murray Bodo, OFM

Music: Josef Raischl, SFO
Choral arrangement: Josef Raischl, SFO, David Dargie

God a-lone is kind, in-no-cent, pure.

From Whom, through Whom, in Whom is all par-

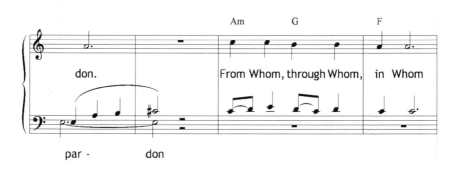

don. From Whom, through Whom, in Whom

par - don

is all grace.

From Whom, through Whom, in Whom

From Whom, through Whom, in Whom

is all glo - ry.

HIDDEN TREASURE
Translation and commentary by Frances Teresa Downing, OSC

Third Letter of St. Clare to St. Agnes of Prague (1238)

Again we are shown the riches which God has prepared for those who love. These words beautifully express Clare's deep conviction about the innate goodness of human nature and the treasure that we bear within us, often without realizing it.

In the field of the world in hu - man hearts lies

hid the trea - sure of e - ter - nal love.

In the field of the world in hu - man hearts

lies hid the trea - sure of e - ter - nal love.

text: St. Clare of Assisi
music: Josef Raischl, SFO
translation: Frances T. Downing, OSC
choral arrangement: Josef Raischl, SFO, Dave Dargie

Third Letter of St. Clare to St. Agnes of Prague (1238)

Clare reminds Agnes that she is one who gives joy to the angels because she is loved by Christ. Again this comes from Clare's letter of encouragement in which she works to rekindle Agnes' enthusiasm. At this time Agnes was struggling with the papacy to allow her to follow Clare's way of life, and she was experiencing conflict between her call from Christ and her call from the Church.

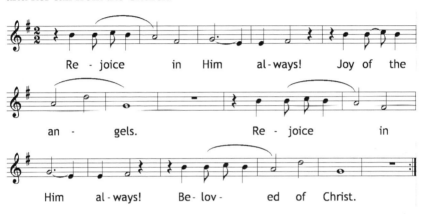

Text: St. Clare of Assisi
Translation: Frances T. Downing, OSC

Music: Konrad Raischl & Josef Raischl, SFO
Choral arrangement: Josef Raischl, SFO, David Dargie

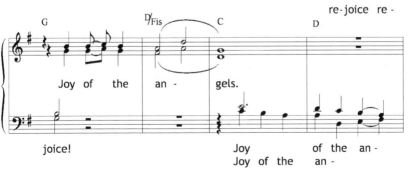

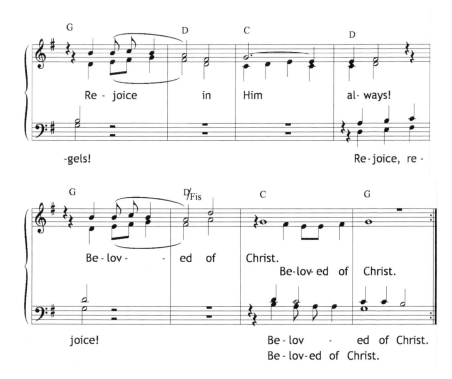

Re - joice in Him al - ways!

-gels! Re - joice, re -

Be - lov - ed of Christ.
Be-lov-ed of Christ.

joice! Be - lov - ed of Christ.
Be - lov-ed of Christ.

JOYFUL HOPE
Translation and commentary by Frances Teresa Downing, OSC

Third Letter of St. Clare to St. Agnes of Prague (1238)

This third letter of Clare was written to encourage Agnes; it beautifully defines the contemplative vocation as one to 'raise up those who are falling.' In the Latin the meaning is clearly one who raises up from beneath, an expression of the lowliness which is part of true minority.

By God's own grace no clouds can dim my joy.

Text: St. Clare of Assisi

Translation: Frances T. Downing, OSC

Music: David Dargie

Choral arrangement: David Dargie

By God´s own grace no clouds

can dim my joy.

additional voices ad libitum:

can dim my joy.

by God´s grace

by God's grace.

LOVE HOLDING LOVE
Translation and commentary by Frances Teresa Downing, OSC

Third Letter of St. Clare to St. Agnes of Prague (1238)
This is very suitable for Communion when we literally hold the living
God who holds us in being—love holding love. So Clare's words give us
theological accuracy and articulate this wonder in a meditative way.

Text: St. Clare of Assisi
Translation: Frances T. Downing, OSC

Music: Josef Raischl, SFO
Choral arrangement: Josef Raischl, SFO, David Dargie

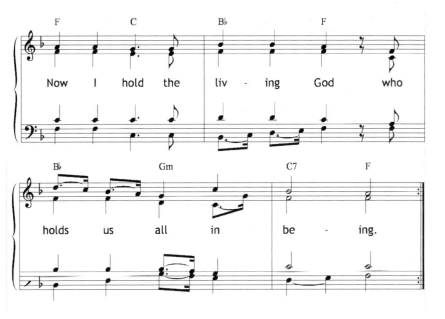

Now I hold the liv - ing God who holds us all in be - ing.

Text: St. Clare of Assisi   Music: Josef Raischl, SFO
Translation: Mary Esther Stewart, Norma Mena   Choral arrangement: Josef Raischl, SFO, Dave Dargie

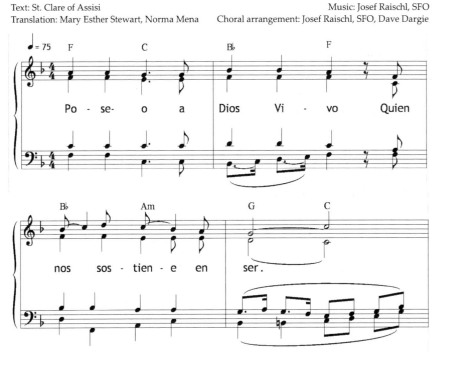

Po - se- o a Dios Vi - vo Quien nos sos - tien - e en ser.

PASCHAL LOVE
Translation and commentary by Frances Teresa Downing, OSC

Second Letter of St. Clare to St. Agnes of Prague (1235)

The love sung in this refrain is the everlasting love of the Risen Lord, so it is very suitable for Eastertide but also for other times when we reflect on the paradoxes of redemption and the place of pain and suffering in our own lives.

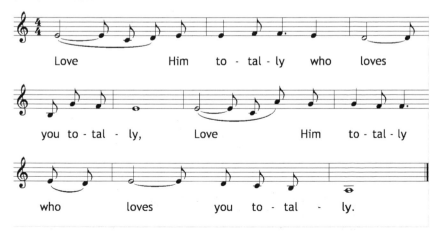

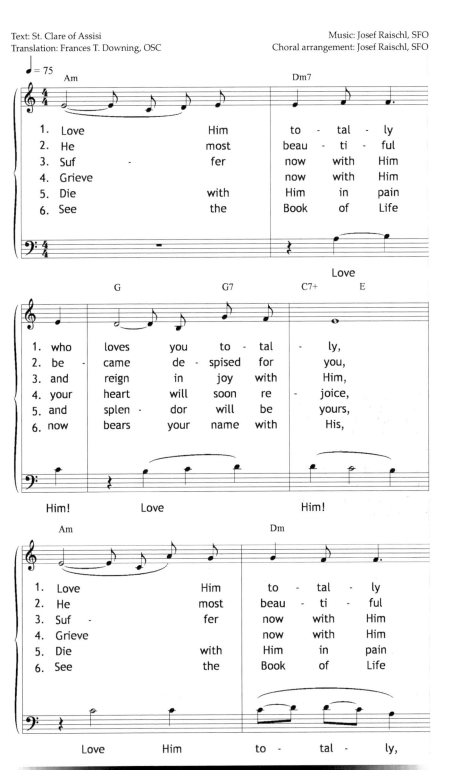

Text: St. Clare of Assisi

Music: Josef Raischl, SFO

Translation: Frances T. Downing, OSC

Choral arrangement: Josef Raischl, SFO

1. Love Him to - tal - ly who loves you to - tal - ly, Love Him to - tal - ly,
2. He most beau - ti - ful be - came de - spised for you, Love Him
3. Suf - fer now with Him and reign in joy with Him,
4. Grieve now with Him your heart will soon re - joice, Him!
5. Die with Him in pain and splen - dor will be yours,
6. See the Book of Life now bears your name with His,

Love Him!

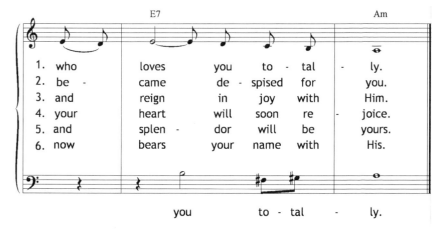

PAX ET BONUM
Commentary by Murray Bodo, OFM

This Latin expression is more than just a greeting. It can be called a summation of Franciscan theology and spirituality. Good is the predominant name the Franciscan gives to God. We are invited to join into the continuum of God's overflowing fountain fullness of GOOD.

Text: Traditional Franciscan Greeting

Music: Josef Raischl, SFO
Round

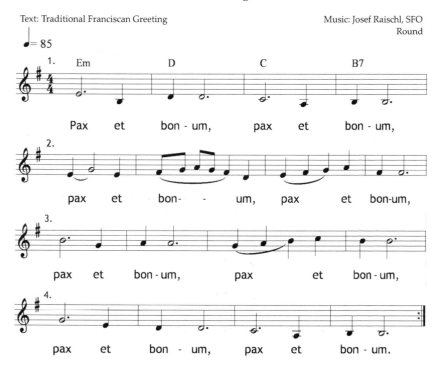

ad libitum 1:

Pax   et   bon - um.

ad libitum 2:

Pax   et   bon - um, bon - um.

SPIRITUAL MOTHERHOOD
Translation and commentary by Frances Teresa Downing, OSC

Third Letter of St. Clare to St. Agnes of Prague (1238)

This song has the lilt of a cradle song, touching as it does on the motherhood of Mary and that spiritual motherhood in which we are called to bring forth Christ in the souls of others.

Once in her bo - dy the Vir - gin of Vir - gins bore the

Word of God. Now in my spir - it I, in my

weak - ness, I bear the word of God.

Text: St. Clare of Assisi   Music: Konrad Raischl & Josef Raischl, SFO
Translation: Frances T. Downing, OSC   Choral arrangement: Josef Raischl, SFO, David Dargie

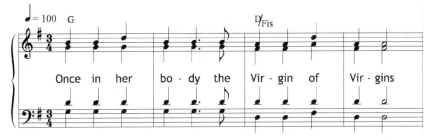

♩ = 100   G   D/Fis

Once in her   bo - dy the   Vir - gin of   Vir - gins

bore the Word of God.

Now in my spir - it I, in my weak- ness

I bear the word of God.

Summum Bonum
Opuscula, p. 90; commentary by Murray Bodo, OFM

St. Francis' THE PRAISES OF GOD *(1224)*

"You are good, every good, highest good." These words from a monograph of Francis on the Holy Names of God remind us of the Muslim 99 Names of God, a fitting Trinitarian articulation of the God Whom Francis and the Sultan Malek al-Kamil discussed together in the Sultan's camp in Damietta, Egypt, during the Fifth Crusade.

Tu es bon- um, om - ne bon - um,

sum - mum bon - um.

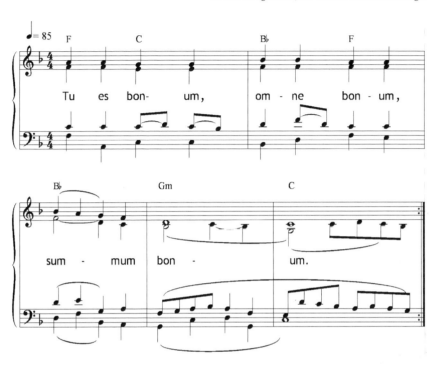

Tu Es Sanctus
Opuscula, p. 90; commentary by Murray Bodo, OFM

St. Francis' The Praises of God (1224)

On Mount LaVerna Brother Leo asks Francis to write some encouraging words for him to help in overcoming temptation. Francis writes the ecstatic prayer that begins with the words, *Tu es sanctus*—"You are Holy, Lord," and continues with an articulation of everything that God is to Francis. "Focus on God and who God is," he seems to be saying to Leo, "and all will be well."

Text: St. Francis of Assisi

Music: Josef Raischl, SFO
Choral arrangement: Josef Raischl, SFO, David Dargie

Tu es sanc-tus Do-mi-nus De-us, De-us so-lus. Tu es

Tu es sanc-tus Do-mi-nus De-us, De-us so-lus.

1. You are strong, grand, most high.
3. You are good, love, wis-dom.
5. You are strength, faith, re-fresh-ment.

Tu es sanc-tus Do-mi-nus De-us, De-us so-lus.

2. You are hu-mi-li-ty, you are pa-tience, beau-ty.
4. You are safe-ty, you are rest, joy.

Tu es sanc-tus Do-mi-nus De-us, De-us so-lus.

6. You are won-drous, you are mer-ci-ful, sweet-ness.

Tu es sanc - tus Do - mi - nus De - us, De - us so - lus.

7. You are tem-per-ance, you are jus-tice, hope.
8. You are de-fen - der, you are pro-tec-tor, meek- ness.

WE ADORE YOU
Translation and commentary by Murray Bodo, OFM

St. Francis' TESTAMENT (1226)

In his final will, written for his brothers shortly before his death, Francis shares how God gave him great faith in churches and taught him to say this prayer, which continues to be prayed by Franciscans today.

We a - dore You, Lord Je - sus Christ, in all Your chur-ches

in the whole world, and we bless You be - cause

by Your ho - ly cross You have re - deemed the world!

Text: St. Francis of Assisi
Translation: Murray Bodo, OFM

Music: Josef Raischl, SFO
Choral arrangement: Josef Raischl, SFO

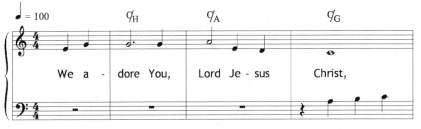

♩ = 100

We a - dore You, Lord Je - sus Christ,

Lord Je - sus

Text: St. Francis of Assisi
Translation: Mary Esther Stewart, Norma Mena

Music: Josef Raischl, SFO
Choral arrangement: Josef Raischl, SFO

First Letter of St. Clare to St. Agnes of Prague (1234)

Clare develops her theme of Christ's love for Agnes and us, returning again and again to the great work He has done for us. This song is arranged so that there are verses for Lent and Easter, but any of them can be sung at any time, perhaps to enter into a time of meditation as the music echoes Christ's coming down into our condition.

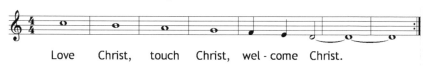

Text: St. Clare of Assisi
Translation: Frances T. Downing, OSC

Music: Josef Raischl, SFO
Choral arrangement: Josef Raischl, SFO, David Dargie

wel - come Christ.

He bore the cross for our sake.

Love Christ, touch Christ, Christ,

4. Have an- y loved as I love?

wel - come Christ.

The Mir- ror calls us as we pass.

Love Christ, touch Christ, Christ,

5. I died, raised high on the Tree,
6. I died, raised high on the Tree,

wel - come Christ.

5. such cost- ly in - fin - ite pains.
6. In sor - row let us re - spond.

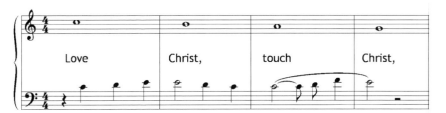

7. Come let us fol - low the Lamb!

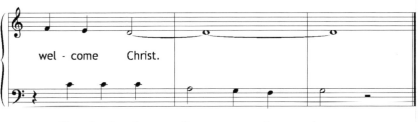

The Lamb in - vites us to joy.

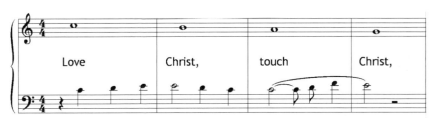

8. Come let us fol - low the Lamb!

Catch fire from His burn - ing love.

St. Francis' EARLIER RULE *(1209/10 - 1221)*

In his *Earlier Rule,* written in 1221, Francis tells his brothers what it is that God asks of us above all else. His words are a portrait of Francis himself and what he tries to do from the time of his conversion until his death in 1226.

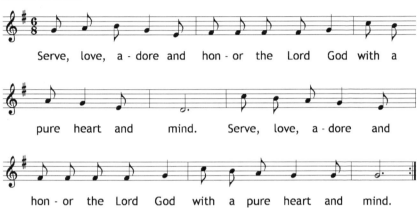

Serve, love, a-dore and hon-or the Lord God with a pure heart and mind. Serve, love, a-dore and hon-or the Lord God with a pure heart and mind.

Text: St. Clare of Assisi

Translation: Murray Bodo, OFM

Music: Josef Raischl, SFO

Choral arrangement: Josef Raischl, SFO, David Dargie

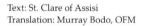

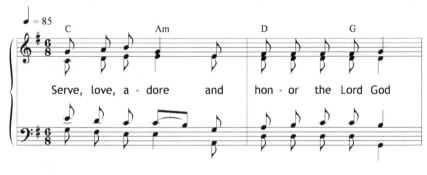

Serve, love, a - dore and hon - or the Lord God

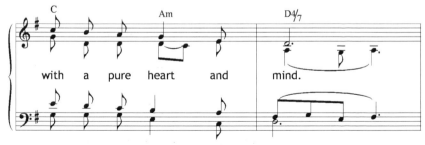

with a pure heart and mind.

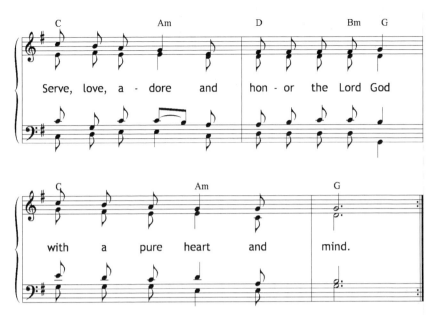

Serve, love, a - dore and hon - or the Lord God with a pure heart and mind.

WITH GREAT HUMILITY
Translation and commentary by Murray Bodo, OFM

St. Francis' CANTICLE OF THE CREATURES *(1225; see page 9)*

Francis ends his great *Canticle of the Creatures* with words that tell us how he served God: the gestures his life made were humble but also grand – large rather than timid and small. He served God humbly but also grandly.

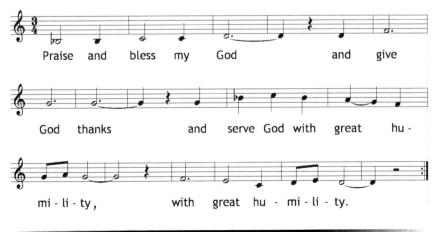

Praise and bless my God and give God thanks and serve God with great hu - mi - li - ty, with great hu - mi - li - ty.

Text: St. Francis of Assisi
Translation: Murray Bodo, OFM

Music: Josef Raischl, SFO
Choral arrangement: Josef Raischl, SFO, David Dargie